FESTIVAL
of ALL
SOULS

Copyright © 2020 Jean Eng

Except for the use of short passages for review purposes, no part of this book may be reproduced, in part or in whole, or transmitted in any form or by any means, electronically or mechanically, including photocopying, recording, or any information or storage retrieval system, without prior permission in writing from the publisher.

The publisher gratefully acknowledges the support of the Canada Council for the Arts and the Ontario Arts Council. The publisher is also grateful for the financial assistance received from the Government of Canada.

Front cover artwork: Jean Eng, "Fridge and Stove" (detail), 2017, acrylic, 12 x 13.5 inches. Artist website: http://www.engjean.blogspot.com.

Cover design: Val Fullard

Library and Archives Canada Cataloguing in Publication

Title: Festival of all souls : poems / Jean Eng.
Names: Eng, Jean, 1954- author.
Series: Inanna poetry & fiction series.
Description: Series statement: Inanna poetry & fiction series
Identifiers: Canadiana (print) 20200329502 | Canadiana (ebook) 20200329561 | ISBN 9781771338219 (softcover) | ISBN 9781771338226 (epub) | ISBN 9781771338233 (Kindle) | ISBN 9781771338240 (pdf)
Classification: LCC PS8609.N25 F47 2020 | DDC C811/.6—dc23

Printed and bound in Canada

Inanna Publications and Education Inc.
210 Founders College, York University
4700 Keele Street, Toronto, Ontario M3J 1P3 Canada
Telephone: (416) 736-5356   Fax (416) 736-5765
Email: inanna.publications@inanna.ca Website: www.inanna.ca

FESTIVAL *of* ALL SOULS

POEMS

JEAN ENG

inanna poetry & fiction series

INANNA Publications and Education Inc.
Toronto, Canada

*To the departed,
in grateful memory.*

Contents

I. WHITE DRAGONS

Night Vision	3
Dragon Nation	5
Blind River	7
Tsao Chun	10
Heat Wave	11
Jitgwa	12
Goddess of the Twin Pavilion	14
Festival of All Souls	15
Taxi-driven	16
Solstice	18
English as a Second Language	19
Bandit Queen	21
Lady Dragonfly	22
Ghost Tigers	24
Sun of a Failed Haiku	25
Dandelion Fields	26
Double Talk	28
Portrait From His Youth	30

Say Goodbye ... 32
For Rent ... 33

II: HER OTHER CHILDREN

Moths ... 37
Crow ... 38
X-rays ... 39
Her Rites Observed ... 41
Nexus ... 42
Wingspan ... 43
A Duck ... 45
Last ... 46
Chill ... 47
Minus 16 Celsius ... 48
White Out ... 49
Forward ... 50
Snake String ... 51
Creatrix ... 52
Snapdragon ... 54
Turkey Vultures ... 55
Climate Thief ... 56
Minerals of the World ... 58

III: BEING SEEN

Bowls of Pain	61
Flight from Earth	62
Grief Mechanic	63
Rx	64
Reunion	67
Hats	68
Maleficent Quartet	70
Sacred Bitch	73
Dance	75
Queen of Wands	76
Deadline	78
Closure	80
Over a Year	82
Never Too Late	84
No City Water	85
Hurry	87
Doctor Heckle	89
Prayer Shelf	91
Stylus	93
Credits	95
Acknowledgements	97

White Dragons

Night Vision

In the hour of the sickle moon
it floats up against the window
like the rag casing
of what was once body
still fluid in blood dialects
cell orchestra
but you can't tell
which shadow warrior
has sent out a form
to knock, knock
against the glass of your soon-dream.
And you think it's the spider plant
on top of the wardrobe
broadcasting at an angle
across the night while a timer
goes on and off some lamp-saving
device in the courtyard
but no wind no breeze
is pushing leaves this far
into organic chemistry.
You stare at the morpheus/obvious
rubbing, bumping its way
on the glass. Long tides flow
up and down swimming pools
thrown on the ceiling.
It's coming forward
stopping on seconds
to agitate
a corner of your dropping mind

the way your mind is now a skylight
and the stars
crack into rings of light years
as the dream catchers open their nets.

Dragon Nation

What the dragon saw
was a trail of smoke
similar to its own breath
after a particularly
exciting day.

THESE PEOPLE MUST RESPECT FIRE.

It wasn't exactly a thought
but a surge of memory
especially when patterns
insinuating the air
traced lines recognized
from its own body.

Dragon-makers lit thin sticks
scented with strong oils
and drew on the surface of air
shapes of longing
rising and curling
like the dance of a great beast
who travelled everywhere
and left behind different
versions of the same story.

THIS IS WORTH SEEING.

Golden eyes scanned the darkness.
Attention turned into myth.

By dawn inventions were born
from almost nothing
and something missing
meeting for the first time.

Blind River

Grandfather sleeps in a box surrounded
by flowers; a banquet—if you didn't know better.
Green bruise on his temple covered with make-up.
Something about bad luck and provocation from
the gods keep stifled tears respectful from a distance.
Silence thickens around his story; a closed casket.
Grandfather's ghost hangs in the closet
like an ironed suit brought back from
the dry cleaner's; a film of thin plastic like
a second skin protecting him from dust ever
after. I know relatives sneak the doors open
to pray inside the wardrobe shrine, benedictions
muffled in jackets, dresses; perma-pressed
sheets, one way to wish him well.
One year, his grandson, who had no license
decided to move the car in the middle of
the cemetery. He crashed into a pole, his
five year old cousin shouting in the back seat.
No one was hurt but superstitions echoed for days
silences declaring: such bad luck such real bad luck
happening on site like that.
A carnival spirit wandered over curious: who is
knocking on cities of the dead?
Catholics and Anglicans rested in that plot
faith shaken out of the ground.
Sleeping forever among strangers, Grandfather is
the only Asian buried there. Is it any different
than never belonging in the bright sunny world
where differences set apart so easily?

Let him eat a while longer, the son whispers to his wife.
They bow their heads: smoke curls in the heat from
joss sticks; a full tray placed in front of the tombstone.
Boiled chicken, cooked eggs, slices of salted pork
three mandarin oranges in a bowl. A feast
to make a ghost hungry. To make a ghost happy.
Thirty years is a long time to live in silence
respecting the dead while their lives
stay an unspeakable language.
What happened that day when the mack truck finally
stopped and passersby gathered, shocked
and curious to watch a Chinese man staggering to
retrieve scattered bills even as he was dying?
Grandfather is on the road out from Blind River.
The satchel holding $500 dollars life savings
breaks open; bills fluttering in the air like
released birds. The driver of the long haul
transport doesn't see him until too late.
A small bunt against the fender, some noise
then—money, floating past his windshield.
Talk about hitting pay dirt.
I have come back through lines of
memory and imagination's sad hope, wanting
to deliver that ghost and us some peace.
He is an omission in our lives, an extra
place set at the dinner table
yet a guest we then try to ignore.
Dead man. Blind River dazzling between the trees.
The whole town lit by a meeting of fire on water.
Most of the people gone to other mining centres
businesses shutting down as customers left.
Bankruptcy, failure. Resilience shredded.

One more round of beginning all over again.
A second hand Chevrolet loaded with possessions.
His wife and daughters asleep in the car.
There is the road and there are more
beginnings that seem like life without end.
Pulling over, he stops, kills the motor. Today
he was one of the last to go having gambled on
waiting, on the turn-around; the restaurant's
empty premise truth's final burden.
Blind River flashing diamonds between the trees.
A mad geography goes from left to right, back and forth.
What he sees ahead is enough to make him bolt:
visions of a duty roster unrolling like a scroll.
The man who supports his entire clan
who intervenes in disputes
who set up his son's café on Manitoulin Island
who sponsors both sets of relatives overseas
takes the knowledge of his own breakage to heart
finally, running blind towards the brilliant river.
Clutching the one chance he believes he has
he is still running even as he runs into
the other side of the world. Paper birds come
alive and money does its magic growing
coming off trees, falling like leaves.
He chases that dream leaving his body behind.

Tsao Chu*

Dust is the room

falling in on itself

like the way the sun loses an inch

shrinking every millennium.

Only the sun is still

a fixture bolted

in mind's sky.

We enter eternity in small ways.

Cat fur tumbles over the carpet

like desert weed.

Nail parings drop. New moons

cross hardwood.

On the rim of a jade plant bowl

leaves pause.

*sweeping dust (trans)

Heat Wave

Humid weather turns
another page from this month.
Breath of a dragon. Even this
can taste of prayer.

How the sky disappears into
lake suspends rule of
one line drawn between
heaven and earth.

The landscape converges
in stillness—heat.

Downtown, a monk counts
his step precious
silence
during rush hour traffic.

The spirit moves
without moving
too much.

Jitgwa*

My mother's cellar hides a secret
storeroom I love to visit:
lair of the hairy melon queen.
She sends me down to admire new babies.
Her voice a disappearing tunnel
from the kitchen upstairs.
Near the alchemy of a stove
her place is steam-bound
smoke-filled and unliberated
as the status quo decides.
But take away the cooking
her ingenuity with food
and joy has nowhere to breed.

Down in the melon chamber, it's braille black.
I grope a small chain for light.
Mounted on wooden crates are prize melons
covered in shrouds of white breech cloth.
From the shadows they bulge in the crease:
zeppelin, belly and beluga; ghost-scented shapes.
To touch them is to feel downy slivers of
fine hair tickle against my palm
and to embrace, half-vegetable swell
near the state of half-beast.

Easy to know why she is proud of them—
they weigh fifteen, twenty pounds.
I inspect each one, tapping for moisture
for clues of thick pulp drying out seeds.
Between strokes of silence
I hear my own breath
counting breaths in the dark.

*trans. Hairy Melons

Goddess of the Twin Pavillion

Below the arch made by two maple trees
the animal in her body
sits quiet as silence
soars through its cathedral.

Psalms bloom in grass grown lush
from soft steps taken
and light bleeds through
spaces the leaves part.

Here it is earth time
star-mapped and shadow-crossed
time when loam and seeds join
to a necklace of bone, breath and prayer.

She draws up to the light.
Radiance cuts her eyes
releasing the dark stare behind it.
She goes back to her copse of roots
bark and branch; feeds
what now comes alive.

Festival of All Souls

Sunrise: a starling on the pavement.
Before dawn scratches through
its membrane of night
a Chinese family gathers in
Birchmount cemetery to
chant names of the dead.

A sphere turns twice.
Music leans against bone.
Ancestors fattened by memory
cross over scented lawns of ceremony
to stand with their tribe.

In the space made by naming
a bird flies through
curious
to be swooping here.
One moment: drinking
from the sky's heavenly faucet
next: seeds of lightning trapped in the throat
and then the singing.
Faces approaching their names.
A sky launched sooner than flight
the bird understands
perfect Cantonese.

Taxi-driven

In another country
where gender is justice
he would not stand for this fire
coming from a woman's belly
her match-lit voice
searing back drafts
into midnight silence.

When she asked him politely
to put the cell phone down
while he was driving
he could have killed her.

Instead—he told her
     just a minute
and waited until a dialogue
concluded with his intended party.
She asked him twice. The meter kept running.

Now, in front of her building
she is trying to burn off his thick accent
to that part of his English
capable of understanding: safety hazards, conscience.

He drives half-way around the world
to pick up his own angry god
stone-walling her logic with incantation.
> I did put the phone down.
> I did put the phone down.
> I did put the phone down.

Now—she wants to brain him
with all of the weather inside her.

Instead, she gets out
takes down the cab number
and slams the passenger door so hard
it sends him back to where he came from.

Solstice

Waves, like white dragons
lunge across Lake Ontario

The sky yanks tarpaulin off
bike and barbecue

flings plastic over a balcony
By the window where

night keens—a painted fan
trembles; its handle inside

the neck of a porcelain vase
Grab the vase and tremors stop

But fans fold drafts into paper
wave the gods who keep

delicate things whole.

English as a Second Language

It was a five point three
according to the Richter Scale.
The little tremor. Few noticed
an agitation so minute, it could
have been a power saw or
the foot of a sewing machine
jogging up its avenue of stitches.
Some however, watched cream
in their coffee stir without a spoon
the spoon, quivering on a saucer nearby
like telegrams in séance.

In a class where English as
a Second Language was taught
students shifted from stumbling over
diphthongs; became toast master generals.
Elocution was crisp; the teacher thought
chicanery and tax receipts the true course objective.

Native speech fled; accents tumbled.
Extensive vocabularies erupted.
People rushed to help unstick
double consonants from the roof
of each other's mouths; loose bits
of good grammar flapped airborne
without paragraph or proper sentence.

Students from Latin America, Indonesia
and Japan recognized the symptoms.

Everyone survived yet mobilized
as a support group. The universal
language was proclaimed
not English—but vibration.
Wavelengths travel faster to the brain
than any degree of fine instruction
speaking of which, the instructor—
briefly ignored during the confusion—
came forward speaking in tongues.

Bandit Queen

In a kung-fu movie, the acrobat outlaw
performs sword dance and somersault
guided by divine instruction.

Frowns gather enough munitions
to discharge thunder from a single
thought. Enter the villain who
takes for granted: this is a lady.

Balanced on one leg
justice kicks rogue ass
over Hunan Province.
The village retrieves its grain.
Children, freed from collateral
resume childhood again.

Women, released from feet
neatly shaped into hooves—
are taught how to wield
long poles tipped with blades.

I'll trade scenes with her:
one act of power enacted
beyond conceivable degree.
Anywhere but here, inside
this trembling body. Alone
on midnight avenue, I clutch
house keys too early for home
wondering, under a streetlamp's dull
moon, whether I'm being followed.

Lady Dragonfly

(after Madame Butterfly)

Psst, Cio-Cio San—come here.
Don't trust that sailor.
It ends badly; I saw the opera.
Marry him and you commit
suicide on the international stage
complete with a full orchestra.
Your grief could slice bone; but worse?
You sing about it in glorious pitch.
Karma dictates that people will buy
tickets to watch you do this over
and over again. Is that what you want?

Japan, with its delicate flavours of
ceremony will entice him to
sample all blossom and fruit as
refuge/reward from the navy.
There's more to living than waiting
three years for a married man who
only returns to collect your son.

Become a martial artist instead.
Devote three years towards
learning stealth acrobatics.
Train in weapons like *nunchaku* or *sai*.
Practice throwing the poison stars
just in case you never know when to
defend your honour from those who

expect abandoned wives to be sport.
Quash this potential for a tragic heroine
by turning Madame Butterfly into
Lady Dragonfly: the geisha-ninja warrior.

Tell the maid you intend to pine
nights away in the garden for
the scent of his hand on your face.
Then sneak off to ambush bandits
if they bother peasant or village.
Paint your shadow like a brush of sumi-e
ink through the streets of Nagasaki.
Haunt criminals with their own
imagination. Leap between young
girls and danger; show them how to
snap-kick wearing a kimono and *geta*.

When that letter arrives stating:
he wants his child but not
you—receive the news with pain
dismay and, yes, everything could
still happen over your dead body.
Except this time you have enough
resources to hobble
anyone's knees should they try.

Ghost Tigers

To prevent a fear
growing larger than myself
I envision this pride of ghost
tigers: Budo, Bantu and Bella.
Bhindi, Bartok and Bohdi.
They emerge from different
countries: world-wide security.
"B" words chosen for the drum-
stroke rhythm of each name called.

One escorts me from the bus stop
at night; patrols range outside
the house. Two hold down the roof.
Others sniff out and hunt small
dreads living in the basement.

Fear provokes their friendship.
They require little food:
I decide what sustains them.
For this I am worth protection.
They eat only what Fear creates to
gnaw at me. Those luminous jaws
barium-injected muscles stalk
terror and its wild, sad legions.

Sun of a Failed Haiku

Awake I found my
self alone on the other
side of a huge bed.

Everything I
kissed wanted to kiss me back.
I must be a god.

Lowered my head to
rest on the horizon's desk.
Thought about a nap.

Dissolved in the lake
like common seltzer. The sky
squeezed my oranges.

Dandelion Fields

That summer, the children disappeared
once a day into dandelion fields. You'd come
out the restaurant back door, scan
the ellipse of North Channel harbor; grease
stains and vinegar clutching your apron.
You knew they stared back. Which one to select?
Hard to tell if game champion wins your
attention first or stays hidden from view.

Signals broadcasted between
their playground and you. But
exclamations of dandelion
interfered with: *look-at-me
over-here, you-can't-see-me* thoughts.
Blowball, lion's tooth, cankerwort—all
these words described by one yellow.
Each child also blended yet unique.

Diners complained with mouths
full of burgers and chips about
the sight of young bodies sprawled so
freshly undead beyond the guard rails.
Their small town minds paced over
how often concern had to be
yanked away by annoyance
every time they saw prone children.

Some days, you missed having
skills of English assigned to your
eldest. You'd pick her out first
watch how quickly she returned.
His father gone, your son tumbled
forward rolls away from his boredom
with the game, not staying
long enough even to be seen.

But one child you chose to leave
blinking among the shaggy flowers
since nothing would break your heart
more than to take off her sky.
She'd fall asleep—golden anniversaries
everywhere—wake up and find sponge ball
buttons, a penny: things no one else would
notice unless they were close to her eyes.

Double Talk

My mother practices English
while I test my Chinese.

Don't speak too much in public, she advises—
you sound five years old.

Between pidgin English and execrable
Chinese, we manage conversations.

How to spell cheesecake? Eglinton Avenue?
Talk English.

How do you say in Chinese…

You'd think we were foreigners
stranded in each other's country
learning the customs badly and in
need of a good dictionary.

How spelling Liberal? Conservative? Communist?

When people go up to the mountains
visit dead relatives and have a picnic—
what's that called again?

L-I-B-E-R-A-L. *Ting Meng.*

It goes on like this; has been for years.
I could've studied Cantonese and she did try
English as a second language. But
when dialogue and vocabulary serve
back and forth; the exchange creates
more than just information.

How are your feelings? If your feelings fine
come home, and I will make you
my beautiful soup.

Portrait from His Youth

In his childhood, the villagers
said nothing when they fell
over dead, seated at tables for
banquets that never came.
They lost to body memory of
how day was broken into meals;
believing that rituals, surrounding
a habit could trick what was missing.

He espied from a window
migrations of the dead on
shoulders of countrymen who
collapsed, became the next statistic.
Wealth was a grandmother who
ordered bags of ration, carried
down thin streets to his family.
Her descendants endured the war
subsisting on rice gruel.

To date, he refuses goods by
country of origin, except for
cameras—where he concedes
the inferiority of other brands.
How he avoids global occupation of
enemy stereos, appliances and tools
without cringing below echoes of

munitions rain, comes from the same
place that knocks him off the couch
laughing. He recalls details of his
youth, as if they were comedy, a joke.

Years may heal history, but
this too is truth: those who
survived fantasies of elusion
concealed themselves behind
drapes not everyone could afford.

Say Goodbye

Listen. The border winds murmur
your longing to believe their
presence, evidence of a loved one.

The brush of a soul's wing
journeying through its ever after.
Then the light. It's warmth

covers your body, tempts all
the hope-lust that hasn't been
dulled by grief: this could be reunion.

But it's only wind and sun and so much
space. Neither angel or guardian
spirit danced the elements for your sake.

So you scatter the dust of what is truly left
under the nearest tree; grant carbon
compounds and biosynthesis their rites to

green your own survival. Nothing else.

For Rent

Her father declines an apartment.
In Cantonese, the words "four" and "die"*
differ only by tone or pitch.
Choose this unit and might as well
rent a funeral home, he says. Despite lake
view, access to Chinatown, his favourite
coffee and donut shop waving across the street—
he dreads bumping into ghosts.
Tenants pass by the open door; carry
enough groceries to sustain the living.
Too late: he's already
pronounced this the dead floor.

She samples the cadence and variety
of each word: how one lifts the palate
while the other dives down her throat.
The apartment spins, but it's only
father's hand waving in her face; a ward
against premature summoning.
She wants to assure him—yes, the puny
number may invoke a homicidal homonym
but the only spirits lodged in this room
reek of a bleach-swabbed floor.
However, if rectangles of a coffin ensure
the dead remain remains— what of the unburied?

Panic reels her in every direction.
She flaps her arms to shoo
the unwanted or misguided

back through corridors of ether.
You think ghosts are chickens?
her father asks, both of them
race-walking to the elevator.
Imprints of their leave-taking
linger behind. They make certain
everything is left exactly as it was
found; their exit distinguished by
what was never disturbed.

sei—four
 séi—die, dead

Her Other Children

Moths

One day lifts out all the routine days.

Wings, gentle as morning candle

fly through the bedroom.

Nests of argyle deep inside

the sock bureau. The threads of

chewed hose, heels and toes

flutter as the whole world

bends to fill in

gaps with a quickening.

Crow

Dour as any warlock
he stomps roof tiles
each step towards sky-dancing

He hacks mornings off
with those blades in his throat
jerked stutters out of my cat

Breakfast is smeared
with jam and cavil
Earl Grey tea salvaged
bits of peace with
essence of bergamot

From his beak the world
dangles upside down
The hierarchy of creation
emptied
over its own myth.

X-rays

This picture of my cat shows everything:
large flat lung with clouds and branches
heart pressed towards bone

Stretched like a yawn or
the anatomy of a smile, she
curves one end of the film to
the other, those neatly stacked
organs curving along with her

According to the vet
they didn't have to use anesthesia
and the staff managed to
keep all their limbs

I am proud of the beautiful
shot she lets them take of
ingredients that make up a cat
Her legs opened like louvers
soft belly exposed to
prying eye of the power lens

At night she comes on the bed
kneads the blankets to
seek places on my body
where it is smooth and she can
ride invisible waves

Measure by heart and mine
is bigger than hers per square inch.
But with prognosis ahead
her small heart still
covers mine when I hold her

If we put our hearts together
maybe we can push on faith
knocking behind one wall to
get through to the other.

Her Rights Observed

Crowded on my patio, they know
one of their own is leaving.
Ginger tom paces flower bed.
Deaf albino on the doormat.
Grey tabby sniffs clay pots for
mouse-scent, left-over piss scent
then settles on the walkway.

Old choir who hissed, spat—then
jettisoned flags of ammonia.
In stealth, the same tribe she
snarled at, bit, and swiped from
her domain—now escort or closure?

The one true wildness retracts all
skirmishes. They will lick and rinse
her spirit, ululate as she crosses
the grey beach. She will run
faster than she ever chased them.

Afterwards, they will no longer
visit the courtyard; as if her
absence finally drove them away.

Nexus

When I am a cat
I tiptoe across the room
wedged between our spare lives.
Grey sand covers the floor.
I sniff a lapse in scent
open my mouth but
swallow nothing, not even
what's next to you.

My turtle life drags me
towards the meromictic lake
dangling in front of
everything I cannot hold.
You return but keep me waiting.
If you must, drink first—then
leave again. I will pause
near any wrinkle of water.

As a vole, I dig
tunnels the length of
sound from ear to
underworld. I hear stones
crack. My small voice
whistles: *you are safe*.
Your laugh is a thousand
seeds, but still your mind's listening.

Wingspan

Riding the Spadina 510 streetcar.
A fruit fly and I both gaze out
the window; my reflection on its
destiny: born to expire the birth day.
Twenty-four hours spooled
around that single route from
Union Station up to Bloor Street.

And what time is it—childhood's
dot of consciousness? Perhaps
youth, in frontier exploration of the only
home it will ever know. Or does
the hour recede awareness of two
antennae, a thorax, abdomen? The last
taste of glass which was never water.

Without warning, I'm in love
with the gaudy tenderness of orange
seats, their resilience in spite of
depression. I grow fond of rows
fitted with heads and shoulders.
Hands, clasped around a pole
support my affection for chrome.

How right day becomes—
sheaves of its news already

folded and discarded in
sections throughout the car.
We descend towards the underpass:
every bell and rustle, iron screech
commends itself towards the living.

A Duck

sleeps alone on the lake
Gale winds toss; her folded body
skims over waves as if
nothing matters except this

good moment to stop the world
and shut off time; stormy
weather and a season's
penchant for grief no more
or less important than a nap

Give us hope and grace
disguised as birds to
carry us through this world
Adrift on heaving waters
feathers cover a small heart
beating against everlasting arms.

Last

Autumn winds shiver
the leaf that must fall but won't.

A blind dancer learns
choreography.

Nothing to follow. Only
sound: one hand clapping.

Chill

It's not so bad, you think.
Parkas brought out of storage
now justify their wolf trim.
Boots, water-proofed in autumn
more welcome than hindsight.
But cedars genuflect from burdens
assigned by too much snow
and missiles drop from stealth eaves.
Austerity tunnels in places where
you failed to make peace with circadian
rhythms by praising all weather.
Forget about trying to love.
It only declares love's absence.
Fatten first on desolation; then
subtract towards cold beauty.

Minus 16 Celcius

On this night of winter
random angels descend
like the one your body left
waving on snow.

The lake grinds its own ice.
Plate sheet, sutures and drift
build each other and a stone
suspends the process of sinking.

Breath blows crystal: variations on
a cloud, snow squall or plume.
You take these impressions home
but they arrive before you. On
glass, frost sends white on white
invitations to your own silence.

White Out

Birch trees, white-washed in
fields of snow, glide silhouette
and shade underneath hues of
porcelain, ivory, and cream.

Angels on holiday sky-dive
for sport; dent and scrape
their wings, crashing into
solids mistaken for light.

Impressions left by hallelujah
free falls—wave on the ground
below; dissolve before the next
influx of headstands.

Forward

The first flame-thumping robin.
Nature is never so sweet as survival.
We've crept out from underneath
opiates of hibernation to blink at
luck, shining without a full sun.

Last year's nests remain
cupped between whiffs of cedar.
Porcelain shard, hollow membrane
the undelivered prayer
moistens the mouth again.

By the time our spirits return from
hitch-hiking once across the park
we remember what it was like
never to feel this hidden.
Our future hands hold round
smooth exclamations.

Snake String

Branches lying on the road
become fluid, trickle into scrub bush.
The snakes of Drunk Man's Hill
migrate out of dreamtime
witness a quiet child.

She cuts herself
a length of white string
chants a private word; then
slithers the string everywhere
childhood has yet to leave.

She comes out of herself in each
string-dragged place, pushing off
the smell from her parents' diner
deep-fried in her clothes; scatters
any need for books, toys, or companion.

The long string glides across
necks of grass, tangles
in a boysenberry bush: her
face, smeared in black
juice, her mouth filled with fruit.

Creatrix

You don't love this earth until
you've met her other children. Once
established, they mock your attention.
Bindweed strangles daylily, twines
from stem to neck; both flower and cord
groping towards the same sun.

You admire crown-shaped blossoms
produced by fritillary bulbs, yet retch at
garlic-ammonia fumes they emit
to contravene their majesty. And how
about delicate ferns, macerated with
poison? Welcome to the touch—
a handful of itch for your pleasure.

You gape at zucchini leaves; a parody of
shields, marshaled into advance
formation. Hordes you never planted
besiege the property—crouching
towards vegetable domination.
You half expect them to roar 'Freedom!'

And here, two-headed tomatoes
split and ooze brown juice. All that
Vitamin C parboiled into dirt soup.
Recycled, naturally, but
what the devil will cough up where
such abominations fell? Good
care in service to good growth
amounts to nothing when the damned
also thrive in conditions enjoyed by
cherished blooms. It's life; eat, eat.

Snapdragon

In memory of Betty Butler

My neighbour identifies her plants in Latin.
Don't know if this unlocks the seeds—
whether that's the secret for
her lavish blooms: the power of
naming, an incentive to life just as
much as earth, water or light.
I want the language of gardens to be
simple like bluebell, sunflower or tiger lily.
Hello instead *Campanula, Helianthus*.
Greetings *Lilium lancifolium*. Waltz
and quick step these words across
my tongue, but why would anyone say
Antirrhinum? Snapdragon. Easier said.
Pity the *Antirrhinum*—who seem to
have a nasal condition: vowels,
outnumbered by consonants only
decongestant spray can relieve.
Give me pink dragons; their delicate
jaws. Bend down to admire them; no
proboscis will be at risk, but at least we
understand the implications.

Turkey Vultures

Between April and November
they soar on dihedral wings
steered by current and thermal.
The escarpment of balsam fir
Sitka spruce and pine, blurs into
khaki patterns. Doesn't matter says
the guide. If it's food, the birds notice.

A migraine drums in this heat.
Voices from the tour group
escort me to a stone bench.
I lie below crisscrossed
branches, close my eyes.
Drafts of resin, mulch and sweat
drift in and out of nausea.

Too late. Too good
a parody of dead meat.
Back into my body
I slam, while the belly of
an eclipse hovers, ready to
devour what the earth
has yet to swallow.

Climate Thief

June behaves more like
November as vortices churn
the sky. Our city darkens, pelted
by ice beads. Street lamps turn on
mid-afternoon—then bars
of light strobe through clouds.
Vanished heat returns.

The temperature spikes so
often we sleep like preparations
for fall: deep, hunkering, and padded.
But awake, compulsions rise to
finish, gather and clean as if
everything left undone
now—will be too late.

We can peaches yet to bloom,
remove air conditioners
never installed
rinse off beach towels
covered without sand.
Quit wearing sunscreen
no one's bothered to apply.

Above us, cormorants
flap backwards out of

sight, deforming the air
with empty Vs.
Monarch butterflies remain
on vacation at
their Mexican hotels.

Body memory has been
rewritten so often, we slip
ourselves genetic codes, designed
for contingency. Our hands refold
origami napkins flung into bushes
then clear off leaves
tabled on the longest day.

Minerals of the World

Soft as stone
patience takes time
carves out human
features in the grain.

Reflections from an onyx eye
returns one everlasting stare
through the skull of time
back to the radiant point of origin.

What holds the eye scans
its own image. In the body—
iron, copper and zinc thickens
blood: water drawn from the stones.

Being Seen

Bowls of Pain

My mother, back from Florida
brought me shells and pebbles
from the ocean, scooped
in an old mayonnaise jar.

That night I dreamt a group of women
passed around bowls of pain:
stones soaking in water.
Take mine, said one—*Here's another*—
and it went around in a circle.

Each woman held the grief
and wept the sorrow of another
as if the company of so many tears
would recollect an ocean.

Flight from Earth

This is what it is like:
a woman hears sound
coming out of her mouth
the words making shapes.
Yet she is standing a few feet away
a voice going on without her.

Grief Mechanic

If you are going to be sad
best do it on a sunny day
while light washes the living
room and shadows from
leaf and branch ripple every
wall and curtain. Here you
have the option to decide
if beauty dissolves without
any loss of radiance; watch
whether it glows and glows
even through rain.

Rx

Pain is never funny—oh no.
Certainly not your own
when it stalks your body
every night
licking pools of sleep.
Mornings you wonder
why your throat is parched.

Quick relief sought in
perfume samples, torn out of
magazines. Free aroma-
therapy if you snort
any that contain oils of
lavender, citrus or mint. But
you collect them all in a shoe
box: scents kicked and bruised
together. More pain, no gains.

Definitely not amused by
a friend's torment while
random pins and needles
throb up, then down meridian
highways inside her flesh
even though she describes
herself as one mother
porcupine in a bathrobe. No point—
sorry, no joke in making
fun, let alone puns.

Straighten the face.
Salt that smile. When co-workers
bend in unison to
retrieve scattered papers
on the floor, never mind
that snap, crackle and pop
no longer alludes to name
brand cereal but one hallelujah
chorus of ungreased joints.

Let us brainstorm—not
too hard, it might hurt—on
protocols of etiquette towards
those who suffer from
their aches. Let us endure
sensitivity training; correct attitudes
language and demeanor
especially towards diverse
cultural groups when they
don't complain, but we know:
their backs hurt too.

We'd be qualified to write
books or manuals; create
a social media presence for
titles such as: The Global Guide to
Saying Diplomatic Things
When Someone is in

Constant Physical Agony.
Pain for Dummies.
Pain Is Not Just
French For Bread.

Reunion

Only recall a few
classmates from high school.
The girl who teased
orange juice over my head
remains forever in Grade 10.

She's trapped in Lunch Room
tipping her glass
back and forth like the time
she couldn't stop before
liquid splashes my hair.

Everyone saw me turn
grab the drink
and hurl what was
left of our best
friendship in her face.

She stands there, eyes closed.
Skin and blouse gleaming wet.
Yet I'm the one who can still
taste the tang of oranges
on a speechless mouth.

Hats

At thirteen, she fears the fashion
police even though blunt, Canadian
winters shove against her body.
Glass tears and nose-drip
chattering teeth—the accessories
to crimes of burst nylons or
welts left by fishnet stockings.

I know she's mortified to admit
protection from nature's elements
as surely as ice will harden
wet, uncovered hair. We need
a coterie of hat-bearing saints or
guardian angels established
before onset adolescence.
They should arrive between tooth
fairy and curfew; grab notice
each year by hoarfrost when
heat starts sneaking off her head.

Santa Fedora, Mère de Cloche, Blessed
Virgin of the Kerchief—please loosen
designer labels affixed to young girls.
Restore circulation to their senses:
divert toques and bonnets away from
sneers. Disguise yourself as a movie
star, famous athlete or musician.

Toss free caps to a crowd like luck
landed on a student budget.

Model parkas in teen magazines—
wear the hood. Confirm the ultimate
rule of cool: that people who wear
hats are hot—enough to avoid pneumonia.
Befriend and ally with her
youth; she can't stop
staring at the world and how
much it stares back.

Maleficent Quartet

1.

Something has bled
FLED
from my veins
each drop quieter than the first.
NO. No more.
I say no more of these hand-held smiles
the corners fixed with pins.
I want exodus. I want that body
to know why she is leaving.
The mirror waits for the usual question
but I don't care anymore—who is the fairest
what land this is, the stupid answer.
I am proud of horns
spiraling out of my head
hardly the trick of beauty parlours.
This cloak, sewn from solitary nights
rampant with thoughts, dreams and conspiracy—
it shall comfort me.
I wrap its shiny rubber fabric
around a landscape howling in rocks and wind.
I go through the domain of this, my country
one eye impaled on fairy tales.

2.

Yes, I pleaded for audience
but who would listen to

a woman gnashing on boulders
swept grey with the mourning
of old funerals?
I draw sharp collars to my chin
while absent lives forage in the dark
looking for souls
incarcerated with their names.
Young heroes, eager for milk-skinned princesses
charge by, gallant, executive
their dreams entombed with castles
promising fully sexed virgins.
Yes I can be the dragon
to end all these tender moments
spitting fire on love poems
written on scented paper;
chomping on roses.
Did you think I'd ignore the real story?
Facts, pointed as these horns
rise up from graves of fantasy
rise from my magic scalp.
I've been there
and yes, I've always been here.

3.

I sit and offer her tea as I
would any guest
and maybe—there are still
lemon cream wafers in the fridge—

but I can hardly entertain a ghost:
hair writhing over china cups
eyes stoppered with rage.
She quietly steals over
keeping that look
and somehow fits into me.
I slowly travel down
with her past the upholstery
down to the floorboards
snake down past pipes of plumbing
into layers of earth where her nesting
place lies, germinating in the loam.

4.

There is a place where I watch you.
A river separates us.
But I can still see you pacing, wary
cloak grasped at the throat; those eyes.
I stand quiet as breath allows.
I have now appropriated antlers for my cause.
They make you twitch in recognition.
The winged ones drop
feathers down my arms.
This mantle matches yours.
I can now choose sky but today
I would stay here, across from you
warming the banks with my feet
witness
while water flows between us.

Sacred Bitch

I want gods to bare their tits
jamboree on holidays
fall off stone slabs laughing
have a decent meal
without our flesh

I want them to shop for bargains
at flea markets, haggle in good
faith with a vendor
flip coins in the fountains of
other peoples' temples
then admire the goldfish

They can screw themselves but
please, practice safe sex
We don't want any more unwanted
gods filling up humane societies
asking for charitable donations

If the gods cannot be found in our
mothers' hands, they can leave
god-riddance, go back
to the hole in the universe
where they came from
to the mother of all gods in there

I want petty gods to know
they are being watched.
Their money is no good here
especially if they don't pay better
attention to themselves

Dance

This dream of dancing takes over
the one about flying
Look down and you're still airborne.
What holds you up no longer
escapes from danger or pursuit.

All exits grow scenic: ballroom
tiles lay down a moveable floor
ribbons of light follow
every arc and turn your
body writes like postscript.

You step back on the world to
dance the living room:
magnetic broom swing dips
underneath a sofa
dust rags twizzle over books.

The percussion of your own heart
cha-chas against a reluctant
cat who prefers you staid.
Still you are happy to be reminded:
you can be happy. The ground
remembers your feet.

Queen of Wands

It's only a stick. Really.
I expected power to lick my
hand like more than benediction
more than birthright—a whiff of
scorched wood at least—
accompanied by drum roll.
This wand delivers nothing but
memoirs of enchantment.

Last employer? A majorette who
twirled an overqualified baton.
What she did on the football field
a better show than the actual game.
The stick cartwheeled and pitched
spells at random—look at that score.
How could I cast from a wand already
gorged on cheers and applause?

Then there was Maestro; he never
understood why Continental Symphony
Orchestra retired after he conducted
Beethoven. Horn players blew out their
lungs. Stage crew had to slip
flat end screwdrivers underneath
chins of a String Ensemble
just to remove the violins.

What could I possibly offer
compared to touchdown
fever and arpeggios?
I point this wand and somewhere
there exists an incomplete set
of chopsticks, potential
hair adornment or
future stake for tomatoes.

Deadline

Must saw wood, hammer nails
pull and staple canvas over frames
before arthritis locks up my joints.
Best record ideas for future
masterpieces in thumbnail
sketches before memory loss
arrives like a suitcase left on
my porch without tags.
Can't have me holding a paintbrush
only to comb my eyebrows with it.
Might as well loosen all the jars now
while my arms remain free of dystrophy
sclerosis and other ailments people
have that I could contract by association.

Should buy another cabinet, sofa,
chest of drawers—in advance of
need: everything assembled and ready
by the time old furniture expires.
Could bully the mattress down to
the garbage room— anger fuelling
what muscle tone lacks.
Bed is only three years old but
good to do this now while
grunt, push and shove still follow my
instructions. I'll sleep on a yoga
mat—won't have far to go if
I collapse from stretching.

Must examine activities that
require me vertical. Plants have to
come down from the ceiling:
no knickknack, gimcrack hanging
higher than I can reach. Must
give up on this, that and that—
surrender that too. Better bitch
today before I misplace the talent or
cry-me-a-river dries up too soon.

Closure

She leaves the bedroom
door open for the cat.
Other guests arrive
through borders thinned
between night and memory.

A queue begins with the only
man who wanted to marry her
but had to find another wife.
His suitcase opens to a life
they never had. The lost wedding
floats bouquets of white rose and lily
over the outstretched arms
of absent bridesmaids.

They file in according to death date
relocations to Calgary, Vancouver.
Estrangement.
Everyone samples rum-soaked cake
after the flowers descend.
The band they would have hired
plays "Unchained Melody."

Grown children appear tall
as columns, present diplomas
from all their schools.
They turned out well despite
having never been born.
The boy studied environmental
politics, manages a nature
conservancy. The girl became
a nurse. She is pregnant with her
first child—a grandson who will visit
when he too, is old enough to travel.

Over a Year

Baskets of patio geranium extend
blossoms next to our drinks.
Nasturtiums welcome the weather by
adding more leaves while ivy crawls
through holes a silence makes.

I have abandoned ghosts of the one
true love. I've declined the means
to win affection at any cost.
Periods reach the end of sentences
and I allow this meal, shared at
Butler's Café to mediate between us.
Looking into his eyes I am satisfied
with the smile that lives there.

Our last time was New Year's Eve.
Spaghetti and chocolate cake for dinner.
Afterwards, meeting in his den
for one final romp. It was understood:
I cared little for champagne and parties—
he rose off the carpet to roam art bars on
Queen Street. We went separate routes
having spent what we had together.

Am I lonely without him?
Don't regret much—not the dinners
movies, and of course the sex.
If I count backwards from ten
life starts fresh. Before memory is
struck by midnight I would wish
upon him the family he has always
wanted and children genetically
predisposed to kindness.

Never Too Late

Another moment
where a jet of well-being
transpires for no reason.
This happens maybe twice a year.
It was late afternoon, summer.
I was walking from kitchen to
living room, when contentment
arrived and refused to leave.
I tried to dismiss it with
accounts of present luck:
must be the new cat or
pay cheque in the bank;
all that free Vitamin D outside.
Yet that other woman who
normally finds fault with
such lists failed to bribe me
with her melancholy nature.
I understood then the true
nature of enlightenment
despite having never been
certifiably enlightened myself.
I felt almost sad for
Sadness, dear roommate
who now had to endure
an entire day with so
little grievance.

No City Water

At work, the sign: "No City Water"
posted on doors and sinks was
meant for our building alone.
Imagine though: drought in
Toronto—all the plumbing choked
shut, or hissing grey fountains.

Those who never ran forward to
fill bucket, chalice or vessel
would now have to scramble
or make a god of rain.

The sky's indelible hue.
Blame, javelin tossed at
Lake Ontario. It stumbles forward
grabs its waves and hurries them
away from shore. Failure is
a natural resource, unable to
inject relief through city veins.
It gleams, wet and useless while
nobody can wash or drink.

The growing season ripens
public and private effluvia
encouraged by a radiant sun.
One employee hugs her kettle.
Some of us lick our teeth.

Our Malaysian Health and Safety
Officer, who meant to say bottled water
informs us he has water bottles.
And how are we supposed to
eliminate in these bottles?
my Jamaican co-worker
demands, hands on her hips.

Hurry

(For the Information Desk)

The woman with red hair fumes
waiting for her turn in queue.
You feel blasts of exasperation
travel over the heads of others while
a phone rings yet another
scattershot round of
wants and needs—not letting up
even after sixteen jangles.

The man you provide with textbook
civil service has too many questions.
It is hard to pay attention, to
address him at eye-level
and flirt with protocol while
your contact lenses remain
at the other counter
where a loading dock alarm
has just sprung its latch and the keys
to silence this intrusion walk off-duty
in the back pocket of your colleague.

You press a knob in your back
surgically modified as extra vertebrae
and launch yourself out to meet
all demands, faster–harder–better than ever
covering more than one desk
with talent-ridden parts of your body.

Legs zoom towards the cash register
make a sales transaction quick
but you forget to stay in your shoes.
They smoke underneath the computer terminal.
They burn holes in your stockings.
One arm unlocks an extra foot to
pinch keys without pinching
the butt of your colleague, then
cranks over to disconnect the alarm
without disconnecting your shoulder.
You clamp phones in your teeth
jab "hold" buttons with your nose yet still
manage to point someone to the washrooms.

By the time shift is over
there is nothing left
except little pieces of you
dispersed like beads of mercury
that sparkle and glob along
then re-assemble
oh joy
to do this all over again.
When maintenance crews arrive
they look at you and yell: "Smile!"
You feel
like grabbing
their throats.

Doctor Heckle

His experiments on himself yielded
results that made memory
enough punishment for each failure.
Bad jokes grafted onto budget
meetings, protest rallies, or
anywhere he found group assembly:

Knock. Knock.
Who's there?
Robin.
Robin who?
Robin the little guy again.

If an audience scowled
groaned, or stepped
away, the uncontrollable
reflex would lurch; he rejoined by
interrupting others when they spoke.

It's one way of being seen.
Better to rely on comedy
corn, ingested with the belief
that if he laughed at his own
humour, others would too.

Better to risk half moons
dampening underarm
floridity of neck and cheeks
than to suffer an invisibility
attack. Underneath his veneer
of social consciousness lurked
his social misfit, always
ready to bust buttons off his shirt.

Prayer Shelf

Televangelist spreads his arms
like forgiveness is the bird of paradise
released from a caged heart.
He suggests we all say prayers for
those who wronged us; create a ritual
to free ourselves from grudge or antipathy.

I forage through my past to
gather an inventory of fall-out;
taste the avoidance of bad-mouth
when one or both of us believed
an ill power of the other.

Sally O'Mara, Adina Newberry.
Stewart Lebowitz, Lori Mueller.
Gene Wade, Li Leung, Sissy Roberts
Alice Spellman, Tom Baedecker
Hester Jackman and Barbie Donne
in junior high who shunned me
even though she smelled of feet.

Altars designed for each person:
rocks, feathers, pieces of cloth.
Old photos, dried citrus peel—
who knew such dormant
love in the making? Closets
and shelves fill as I find more
people than space to include them.

Can't resent the ones after
all, who cried me, me, me
when I cried "me too."
The wrong soul mate now
treats his wife like the mother
I never was; of course who had
enough nerve then to admit
relief when tyrants quit the room?

Black candles and incense too
for this bully of a stylist in one
Yorkville hairdressing salon or
that plumber, whose attitude was
worse than any toilet. Shrine
for them under a bathroom sink
with all my paper and shampoo.

Won't forget the dentist who
filled a wrong tooth; he said
insurance should still cover it.
Shove him in the pantry next to
honey jar and maple syrup.
That racist bus driver when
I turned twelve, my second grade
school teacher with her curriculum
of dragging pupils by the hair—
holy up and God bless
everyone: you are all mine.

Stylus

At the gallery, a visitor remarks
that my painting of a pen
looks quite phallic:
the lines shown scribbling out
from underneath the nib
obviously a reference to pubic hair.

How could you not
make the connection, she insists.
I want to buy her a shovel or
extend an invitation to
dig in her own dirt.
All I see is pen. And ink.

Instead, I curtain my
face and flip through
memory's catalogue for
instructions or suggestions
on how to validate
different ways of seeing.

Credits

Thank you to the editors of the following journals and magazines where some of the poems (or versions thereof) in this collection first appeared:

"Night Vision," *Contemporary Verse 2*, 21,1 (1998)
"Blind River," *Contemporary Verse 2*, 20,2 (1997)
"Tsao Chun" and "Nexus," *Woven Tale Press Magazine* (2019)
"Taxi-driven," *Canadian Literature* 163 (1999)
"Solstice," *The Dalhousie Review* 93.3 (2013)
"Bandit Queen" and "Hurry," *Rigorous* 2.3 (2018)
"English as a Second Language," "Reunion" and "Closure," *The Nashwaak Review* 28/29 (2012)
"Say Goodbye" and "Climate Thief," *Stand Magazine* 17.2 (2019)
"For Rent," *Grain* 45.2 (2018)
"A Duck," *WomenArts Quarterly* 6:3 (2016)
"Flight From Earth," *Canadian Woman Studies/les cahiers de la femme* 23.1 (2003)
"Maleficent Quartet," *Room* 25.3 (2002)
"Stylus," *Vallum* 12.2 (2015)

Acknowledgements

Thank you all for reading.

Thanks to Toronto Arts Council for financial support in the writing of some of these poems.

My gratitude and appreciation goes to Luciana Ricciutelli, Editor-in-Chief, Renée Knapp, Publicist, Val Fullard, Cover Designer, and everyone at Inanna Publications for allowing my debut collection of poetry to come true.

I am fortunate to have friends and colleagues who are both artists and authors. Thanks in particular to Carol Barbour and Lillian Michiko Blakey for the way words and paint segue back and forth with natural grace and ease. Special acknowledgement to Oriah and members of the first writing circle I belonged to, where I discovered my interest in pursuing poetry.

Finally, thanks to my family who remember and share stories I never knew about or almost forgot.

Jean Eng is a writer and visual artist from Toronto, Ontario. Her paintings have been exhibited in Canada, the U.S. and Japan. They also hang in public and private collections including the Government of Ontario. Her poetry has appeared in literary journals in Canada, the U.S., and the United Kingdom, including *Canadian Literature; Contemporary Verse 2; The Dalhousie Review; Grain; The Nashwaak Review; The New Quarterly; Room; Vallum* and *WomenArts Quarterly.* Her work was also included in a limited edition chapbook, *Lacewing,* an anthology of nature poetry. She lives in Toronto.